Survive Gaming Apocalypse

DIMA KOTIK

Edited by Maria Kotik

SURVIVE GAMING APOCALYPSE

Version 1.00

Turabian: Kotik, Dmitry. *Survive Gaming Apocalypse.* Edited by Maria
Kotik. Cary, NC: CreateSpace, 2012.

MLA: Kotik, Dmitry. Survive Gaming Apocalypse. Ed. Maria Kotik. Cary,
NC: CreateSpace, 2012.

DEDICATION

This book is dedicated to my dear and loving parents, Oleg and Olga Kotik.

CONTENTS

CONTENTS

CHAPTER 1

INTRODUCTION

"We are plain quiet folk and have no use for adventures. Nasty disturbing uncomfortable things! Make you late for dinner!" – Mr. Baggins, The Hobbit

Why a hobbit? Out of all the inhabitants of the Middle Earth, a hobbit is a rather strange choice for the main hero of the great epic, the Lord of the Rings, by J.R.R. Tolkien. Hobbits are weak and small. They are not good with magic. They cannot run fast or climb well. They are terrible swimmers. Most weapons are far too heavy for them to wield, nor are they known for their wits. Even if two of them managed to draw a bow by working as a team, they could not hit an ogre at three yards. Hobbits do not rise to positions of power or authority. They live in a relative seclusion of their settlements, fearful of what might be out there.

J.R.R. Tolkien is a genius. One of the secrets to his great success in art is the selection of a hobbit for a hero. Tolkien has outstanding writing skills, but it is his unsurpassed craftsmanship in storytelling that truly sets him apart. Why a hobbit? Tolkien chose a hobbit for a hero, because we are the least likely candidates for heroes. We spend most of our lives living like hobbits in seclusion of our Shire, focused on the trivial and the mundane. Our striving for achievement impresses only other hobbits, if it attains anything at all. The nagging suspicion, that outside of Shire our great accomplishments are laughable, keeps us chained to our small circle of friends. Yet deep inside we hope that there is a special purpose for our lives. We dream of that destiny to find us.

Our desire for finding purpose and significance sets us on a quest for adventure. That is why we enjoy books and movies so much. They are not merely an escape into a world of surrogate excitement. They truly become a source of inspiration and hope, especially when it comes to religious writings. We want to know and experience more. Hope feeds our imagination and makes us hungry with anticipation. Our understanding of our personal purpose in life is the seat of our moral convictions and our motivation to work. We desire to leave an enduring legacy, and this desire is never fulfilled unless the choice is made of what this legacy is going to be. In fact, most of us will spend at least a third of our lives trying to figure that out. But the quest for significance does not end there. It only begins. Purpose is a moving target. In order to continue to discover our purpose, we crave for adventure.

Modern digital world opened up new areas of exploration. Computer games have now become the dominant form of entertainment in the world that passes reading in terms of hours invested per person. One of several fascinating facts that continue to puzzle evolutionary biologists is the existence of entertainment. The more developed an animal is, the more time and energy it devotes to playing. While playing has some potential evolutionary benefits, it is hard to imagine how animals that play more out-bred animals that play less.

It is equally difficult to fathom why the least entertained people and nations are rather seldom the most productive. A closer look at modern life reveals some interesting observations. Even in tough work environments with 60-80 working hours per week, most of us spend a third of our caloric energy on entertainment preferring it over sleep. A similar curiosity of nature is found in almost all mammals, the majority of which spend 30% or more energy on playing. Even people who have become completely obsessed with work have not done away with entertainment. They have simply made their work their entertainment.

Unless you were born in a place like North Korea, you play every day. The kind and the quality of your entertainment will make a big difference in your life. Variety, moderation, and inclusion of other people are all important when it comes to the question of entertainment. While electronic entertainment has become the most common kind, it is still a dangerous and unfamiliar territory for most people. Because this area is so vast, few know what is out there and what to watch out for. And this is what this book is about.

Who This Book is For

Technology continues to alter the way we live. Developed nations are reaping great benefits of wealth through efficiency that comes with automation. We have the resources to feed, clothe, and shelter every person on the planet. Corruption and apathy are the only two real obstacles in the way of progress. This will be true even if nothing new will ever be invented or improved. Our current technological power is already sufficient to create a better society, if we can get past self-interest. Clean energy and water, exceptional health care and limitless food supply in harmony with nature are all within our reach.

Increasing wealth and productivity through automation is having less influence on the way we work and provide for our needs and much more influence on our leisure and recreation. For the first time in our history, some European nations have allowed the total number of weekly work hours to be less than the total amount of leisure time available to the majority of their citizens. If current trends hold up, at least a third of our time will be spent on electronic entertainment driven by social media. However terrible or wonderful that might seem to you, it is certain that this presents a unique challenge. Chances are, if you are holding this book in your hands, that this digital take-over has already begun in your family. You are crossing the threshold into gaming apocalypse. This book is your survival guide.

You, or someone you know and care about, are becoming entangled with the virtual world. Gaming often becomes a time consuming hobby that puts a heavy strain on family relationships. Having a spouse that likes to play computer games can be even more troublesome. This book is not written to raise alarm and spread panic of the inevitability of our demise in the eternal slavery to the machines. Now that I think of it, the title of this book does sound like ravings of an alarmist lunatic. Take it with a grain of salt. Technology is a powerful tool. You must embrace it and use it to promote virtue, worship, and truth. Technology is also a dangerous tool in careless hands. If you are seeking to understand better what those dangers are and how to deal with them, especially in the area of electronic entertainment, this book is for you.

This book is not meant for settling family disputes or providing ammunition to parents for grounding their kids. I may provide some recommendations, but my main goal is to inform you, so that you will be able to make better choices for yourself and your family in this area regardless of the specifics of your concerns. After becoming familiar with basic components of virtual worlds, we will explore together their benefits and dangers. Next, you will learn how to protect yourself in those worlds, and how to protect your family. By the phrase "virtual world" I mean to say "a computer game," and I will use those terms inter-changeably throughout the book, because the second one is too limiting and a bit misleading. Computer games have become a lot more than just games.

What Makes a Virtual World

Thinking about computer games as virtual worlds is the best way of understanding them. The variety of games is only restricted by human imagination and the strength of computer hardware, both of which are steadily growing in capacity. It is difficult to classify them, because they often combine ideas in unpredictable ways. They also give their visitors a degree of freedom. There are, however, five basic components that can be found in every virtual world. Grasping those components will help us understand and evaluate most games. More importantly, it will help us understand the effects games have on people, both positive and negative.

Interactivity

Interactivity is having an opportunity to make a choice. The choice can be quite trivial between colors and shapes, or it can be a matter of life and death for characters in the game. If you ventured to slay a dragon with a group of companions, some of them may not survive because of the wrong decisions that you made in battle. Interactivity is what sets games apart from movies and what sustains the bridge between the physical world and the virtual. Physical tools facilitate interactivity, which are normally a display paired with a game controller or mouse and keyboard.

In essence, interactivity is freedom. Like any type of freedom, virtual freedom is bound by virtual natural law. Natural law is only bound by the imagination of the one who created the world.

Virtual reality, then, is not just interactive. It is interactive in interesting and often unexpected ways according to the intention of the author of that world. Freedom in virtual reality inherently carries the danger of evil because of choices involved. When you enter this world, you enter the domain of the author, a flawed person, who defined right and wrong in it. The intersection of freedom and danger gives birth to risk and exploration, which are the core reasons why people like virtual worlds. This is also the source of all the problems associated with virtual worlds. We will return to this discussion later in the book.

Agents

Agents are things that players interact with in order to change the virtual world, and there is an impressive variety of them. They often appear as physical objects or characters. In simple games, those might be blocks, tiles, and balls. And in sophisticated games with high levels of interactivity, almost every object on the screen is an agent that can be manipulated in some way. Skyrim, one of the most popular games, lets you steal almost anything that you can lift. The things that you steal are agents, but the characters which own the things that you steal are also agents, and your act of stealing is a way of interacting with them. Agents can be both helpful and harmful to the player. The majority of time in games is spent on interactions with different agents. For example, a rather typical game scene is a repetitious application of the club-agent to the zombie-agents until all is calm.

Monsters constitute the most common category of agents. They are scary and often disturbing, but they are also the closest feature that virtual worlds share with books and movies. Monsters are embodiments of human faults. They exaggerate common human sins and vices. Orcs are our mercilessness; zombies are our gluttony;

vampires are our greed; skeletons are our decay; werewolves are our savagery; ogres are our cannibalism; and dragons are our wars. Defeating the monsters is a metaphor for overcoming sins and temptations. Likewise, agents that aid the player are usually slightly dressed up incarnations of hope, love, joy, peace, patience, kindness, goodness, and faithfulness.

Narrative

Interactions between players and agents shape the narrative of the game. The story can be primitive: the protagonist gains many points and earns congratulations. The plot can also be unbelievably complex with many concurrent threads and unexpected twists rivaling the best of fiction. The narrative of the virtual world is often the main reason why people play computer games, and it is by far the greatest source of enjoyment. Everybody loves a good story!

The most amazing feature of virtual worlds is that the narrative itself is interactive. Choices that the players make may alter the story. Sometimes even the ending of the story can be changed depending on the course of action taken. Such worlds are called "open-ended." Narratives of multiplayer games are even more fertile for imagination, because actions of several players summed up lead the story, sometimes in completely unpredictable ways.

Within this great range of possibilities, standard plot devices of books and movies dominate computer games. Bad guy takes the princess, and a prince must rescue her. An evil scientist is destroying the world, and a hero must stop him. An impostor abuses his own people, and a rebel from a lower caste must take him down. The narrative always carries a moral lesson. Since players influence the development of the story, they can connect with it in profound ways and come under the great weight of the central message. This key aspect of virtual worlds is particularly important for our later discussion of ethical considerations.

Risk

Every decision of the player, however trivial it may appear, involves a gamble. Intended and unintended consequences follow each action. The events that unravel form the setting for adventure that becomes more meaningful at each turn. There is something to lose and something to gain in every situation. The central source of risk in games is usually a strange contraption called the "life bar" or "health bar." It measures points and displays them to tell the player how well he or she is doing. Losing all points usually leads to virtual death by the doom of the "Game Over" message.

Removing the element of risk from the virtual world destroys its entertainment value. The rewards attained in the adventure become meaningless, if nothing was at stake in attaining them. This happens mainly because every good story has a risk climax and falls apart if it is removed. If the prince rescues the princess from a castle by strolling in and out, without having to fight the dragon, he is unable to hold our admiration or even attention.

Exploration

Exploration is simply tasting progress by experiencing something new. It is also a major motivator for reading books, watching movies, and visiting virtual worlds. Nobody would ever want to buy and read a book about their own daily routine, because it would be helplessly boring. We read books in order to experience something that would otherwise be too taxing or impossible to for us try, like another person's adventures. It reads better if another person is a spy or a private investigator. Books, movies, and virtual worlds are bridges that bring us to new things and new people.

In the realms of imagination, where everything is possible, exploration faces a unique challenge. New things encountered must be sufficiently different from what we know to be interesting, and they must be sufficiently familiar to be recognizable. That is why the majority of mythical beasts and pagan gods are stapled pieces of random animals and human body parts. Otherwise, they would not be very intimidating or interesting. As different as virtual worlds may seem to us, they are actually fairly close reflections of the physical reality superficially bent in a limited number of new ways.

Game designers produce art assets and combine them in thousands of ways to create new characters and new scenery out of the familiar. Gigantic worlds are constructed rather quickly, and their makeup meshes instantly with our imagination by juxtaposing old things with new things. Some areas of every virtual world are temporarily restricted to generate alluring mystery. Those areas will become open to the player gradually. Our minds are instantly drawn in the pursuit of this mystery because those worlds resemble our dreams. The best example of that is the world of "Minecraft," one of the most successful games to date, which is made almost entirely out of arrangements of roughly ten different kinds of cubes.

An additional strong appeal of exploration in virtual worlds comes from countless opportunities to satisfy curiosity. When reading a book, if the author does not tell you what is hiding behind a squeaky door, you will never find out. In a virtual world, you may be able to find out. Furthermore, the game will most likely reward you for peeking around and observing the scenery. Game designers, like squirrels, stash something helpful and interesting in different corners of their world for the player to find. They also include slow and boring parts in-between intense action in order to give the players room to explore and to satisfy their curiosity in the vast expanses of their virtual worlds.

Basic Ethical Considerations

The five basic components of virtual worlds, interactivity, agents, narrative, risk, and exploration, together form a fertile soil for conflicted situations. Making ethical decisions in virtual worlds can be a rather complicated task. Understanding this quite well, game designers seem to enjoy purposefully trapping players in difficult moral dilemmas. Facing those tough choices is what makes exploration of the virtual world meaningful and transforming because they are at the core of the game's narrative.

Does it really matter what choices a person makes, if the virtual world exists only inside the computer? There are certainly no immediate observable consequences to making a wrong ethical choice in a computer game, but there is definitely a powerful connection between the game and the player. First, virtual freedom and anonymity may indicate in a limited way what the person is really like when nobody is watching them. Second, continual and careless exposure to virtual worlds can form destructive habits that undoubtedly transfer into the physical world. Let us take a brief look at some of those areas of moral and ethical landmines.

Actor–Observer Asymmetry

Virtual worlds allow players to interact with world agents and each other. By their nature, those interactions can imitate regular human relationships. Every participant assumes a role in the drama of the game as action and dialogue sequences advance the plot, giving fertile ground for an interesting quirk of human psyche called "actor-observer asymmetry." This effect is blame pushing at its core.

In a nutshell, it is our human tendency to explain our questionable actions by appealing to our circumstances and actions of others by judging their intent. For example, if we mistreat another person, we are inclined to insist that our situation guided our actions rather than our personal feelings or choice. But if another person mistreats us in a similar way, we are also inclined to insist that they intended us harm all along regardless of the situation they were in. Ironically, we are much more aware of our personal intentions than intentions of other people.

In extreme cases, this quirk can generate uncontrollable self-pity and victim mentality, when all our actions are blamed on circumstances or other people. Computer games are often set up in a way that naturally gives in to or even promotes actor-observer asymmetry. This is especially true for games in which the player controls a criminal. A heart wrenching back-story followed by several scenarios where you happen to be at the wrong place at the wrong time, forced to protect yourself, are sometimes given as pretext for committing crimes for the rest of the game.

The greatest danger does not reside in those actions per se, but in motivations behind those actions. If this motivation is habitually fueled by reactions based on assumptions about another person's intent, an excuse can be readily fabricated for any heinous or treacherous act. Beware that computer games can be the most powerful promoters of actor-observer asymmetry by perspectives that they assume as their stories unfold.

This effect is magnified by the fact that the majority of characters in virtual worlds that the player encounters are flat. They do not have much of a personality, and they are usually driven by one and only motivation. It is easy to pass judgment on those characters and deal with them as you see fit in a pinch. Real people that those characters may often represent are not like that. They have complex emotions and motivations that are often in conflict. The primitive virtual divisions between good people and bad people cement actor-observer asymmetry and chain our sympathy to our identity. We will discuss this further in the section on racism.

Anti-Hero Phenomenon

A large number of virtual worlds employ an anti-hero protagonist for the main character. He or she is a profoundly flawed hero that wins the sympathy of the reader by displaying courage in the face of impossible odds. Interestingly, one of the first major anti-hero types was born in the epic poem "Paradise Lost" written by John Milton in 1664 in those famous paraphrased words:

> "To reign is worth ambition though in Hell:
> Better to reign in Hell, then serve in Heaven."

Of course, those are the words of Satan in the poem. They have a profound effect on the readers. We cannot help but admire slightly the courage and resolve of Satan in opposing God. Those words capture the paradigm of the anti-hero genre that is becoming dominant in art. Examples are bountiful, starting with mild cases like Iron Man and Dr. Gregory House, and ending with extreme cases like Vito Corleone in "The Godfather," which is still widely considered the greatest movie ever made. We are drawn to the anti-hero types, because we find ourselves in them. It naturally follows that the most popular computer games tell the stories of anti-heroes.

Stories about anti-heroes are not necessarily satanic or evil in themselves. They have tremendous value. The classic story of Samson in the Bible comes to mind. He was a great warrior, tricked by a woman, blinded and enslaved by his enemies. He is a rather disgusting anti-hero in every way, and the Bible makes no effort to give him any positive traits other than his strength. His tragic and repulsive life ends with a last-ditch attack on his captors. Yet, Samson is better remembered than the classic righteous hero Joseph. The ugliness of Samson's story somehow strikes a chord. Why do we secretly admire him?

Tragic events that bring us harm force us to stop and think about deep questions of life. This interruption is just as important as the conclusions we might reach. Answers to tragedy can only be held lightly, because we will not understand the purpose of evil entirely in this life. Thinking about it, however, transforms our character. The anti-hero phenomenon is a twist of classic tragedy genre. Virtual worlds can create redemptive interruptions by taking us into tragic situations, but they can also rob us completely of the benefits by trivializing consequences of choices made or by carelessly turning an anti-hero into a hero.

When there are redemptive qualities in the anti-hero, gleaning them from the story requires having trained discernment and mature stable character. Be careful about introducing children to anti-heroes. A person must have a frame of reference and proper grasp of basic complexities of life in order to understand and appreciate an anti-hero properly. Otherwise, you or someone close to you will be in danger of admiring criminal and violent behavior dressed up in frivolous excuses. And what you most admire, you will imitate.

Subtle Indoctrination

Virtual worlds are crafted by people. Game creators inevitably incarnate their own perceptions of reality, order, morality, and beauty in the worlds that they create. Although this is true of every form of art, virtual worlds have the greatest power to impress and indoctrinate due to interactivity. This power can be an instrument of good or a tool for evil.

Indoctrination is the gradual and subtle re-arrangement of values through interaction with others. It is inevitable when communication and relationship are present. The greatest source of entertainment in games, immersion, is also the greatest source of danger, because participants come into very close, almost intimate, psychological contact with the game creators through their creation. Even if the game does not purport to maintain moral neutrality, it may slip into teaching amorality. Moral vacuum and neutrality do not exist, although morality may not be as apparent in simple games.

There are many games that allow the player to make moral choices and to choose moral development paths. Games that allow moral choices often reward the player equally in terms of game-play regardless of the choices made. Their game experience will alter based on choices, but they will still be able to finish the game and earn rewards of one kind and another. The sneaky lie of such worlds is the sublime suggestion that all moral paths are potentially equal in entertainment value and reward.

The consequences of choices made have an immense power to teach morality. This will be discussed in more detail later in the book. For now, simply note that all games have capacity to indoctrinate and to conform the participant to the nature and laws of the virtual world. This conformity can put you in conflict with the nature and the laws of the real world, because they are often quite different. This is one comical anecdotal example of such indoctrination in the reaction of a child to the death of the family cat: "Daddy, where is the reset button on our kitty?"

Effects on Psyche

The most common misconception among youth regarding

computer games is the idea that what you do in computer games does not matter. Are there no real consequences in virtual worlds? If an activity does not really hurt anybody, why is it a big deal? While it is true that actions have limited consequences in virtual worlds, those consequences bear additional weight on our responsibility to police our own imagination and thoughts. Some things are wrong to imagine or to think or to believe. All our conscious actions are informed by our thoughts, which are conditioned by our previous meditations. It is dangerous to pretend that they are not.

Full extent of psychological influence of games on human mind is unknown, mostly because psychology is a young and undeveloped science. Research on this subject just started to appear at the end of last century. The greatest obstacles between researchers and conclusive answers have been the rapid rate at which games have been evolving and their enormous variety. You will find studies with wildly differing conclusions and few solid recommendations. Physiologists have been simply unable to keep up. There are, however, essential psychological truths known from other areas of study that definitely apply to virtual worlds.

First, what goes on inside your head matters. Dwelling on evil can cause depression, anxiety, fear, and even physical illness. Likewise, meditating on good can increase productivity at work, attract friends, and even aid in physical recovery. Actors are known to experience real symptoms of sick characters they play. Actors are also a high-risk group for substance abuse because of having to emulate negative emotions of the characters they play. Computer games that immerse the player in emotional negativity for extended periods of time can sometimes produce similar effects.

Second, our minds are never fully under our control. Some parts of our brain are autonomous and instinctive. Willpower can be developed with discipline, but impulses and reactions will always precede conscious thoughts. Games, like books and movies, can cause you to entertain ideas that you might not have allowed yourself to consider on your own. As a participant in the story, you may come under influence more powerful than you have been accustomed to. Guard your mind. Although you cannot always fully control what you think and how you think, you can alter your environment to help you steer your thoughts to develop healthy thinking habits. There is always the option to turn the game off and walk away.

Third, our minds are vulnerable to the media. Advertisement industry is built on this basic principle. This is especially true for games because they can include almost any form of art and media in them. There are companies that sell virtual advertisement space by including marketing media inside the virtual worlds. Media is never neutral; it always carries a powerful message that calls for critical evaluation. Nothing should be accepted at face value. Our mind should always be engaged in active filtering of messages. Sometimes this will save you from falling prey to misleading advertisement, and one day it may save you from a deadly suggestion.

Developing Restraint

Restraint is a mark of adulthood and maturity. It is just as important to learn to exercise restraint in the virtual worlds as it is in daily human interactions. Restraint is willful choice to limit personal freedom for a greater good. Some may consider personal freedom the greatest good that must never be restrained, but such line of reasoning leads to error and destruction. At the very least, our personal freedom should not be promoted above the value or freedom of another person. Civil authority exists as an artificial restraint for those who are unable or unwilling to exercise self-restraint in the physical world. In virtual worlds, we have to learn to police ourselves.

The first set of decisions that must be made with restraint have to do with amount of time devoted to gaming. Computer games can be beneficial, but in excess they are destructive like any other good thing. Then, the restraint must be applied to our human desire to entertain self, if this personal fun gets in the way of daily responsibilities or comes at the expense of another person. Finally, our actions and choices in virtual worlds must be limited by restraint in interests of integrity, mental health, and well-being of others.

People are born with limited ability to exercise self-restraint. It can be fostered through personal discipline. If you are a parent, you are obligated to teach your children self-restraint as an adult life skill for their own good and success in life. Virtual worlds are actually a great opportunity to teach this life skill by constraining their freedom at first and increasing it over time. Reward mature choices and evidence of self-discipline by gradually increasing freedom. Be a good example by practicing self-denial and self-restraint in every area of your life. Parenting tips will be discussed in more detail later in the book.

Are Virtual Worlds a Waste of Time?

After reading the list of ethical considerations above, you may start thinking that it is best to stay away from virtual worlds completely and to keep as many people as you can away from them as well. Perhaps you are a concerned parent looking for justification to ban electronic entertainment in your household. In some households computer games should definitely be banned entirely at least for a limited time, if they have consumed the family life. As a general rule, however, prohibiting things for others that are not prohibited by God stunts the moral development of the people involved on the both sides of the prohibition. Undiscerning prohibition short-circuits spiritual growth because it eliminates discernment from our thinking.

CHAPTER 2

VALUE OF VIRTUAL WORLDS

"They who dream by day are cognizant of many things which escape those who dream only by night." – Edgar Allan Poe

Computer games are commonly perceived in a negative light. If you enjoy playing computer games a lot, you might seldom acknowledge that fact in a company of strangers and wait until somebody else brings it up. If computer games are a waste of time, then a person who likes to play games is likely to be considered lazy. If computer games are thought to be for children, then people who play them may also be immature. If you admit in public that computer games are your private hobby, you run the risk of other people thinking that you might have difficulties connecting with the opposite gender and making friends in general. To test the truthfulness of those public perceptions, try putting "avid gamer" as a hobby on your next job application.

Stereotypes can be misleading, but they always have a grain of truthfulness to them. It is not hard to think of a person you know exhibiting those traits in appalling ways. Virtual worlds do have the potential to foster laziness, immaturity, and isolationism. We will discuss those things in the following chapter. But they can also be tremendously beneficial, and knowing what the potential benefits are is essential for making mature choices regarding your involvement in those things.

Adventure

Adventure makes life worth living. Simply put, it is an expectation of a pleasant surprise. And in practice, it is the foundation of every religion, philosophy, and human effort for achievement. Adventure gives purpose to life through anticipation of reward and fulfillment. It is also a vehicle of transformation, in which the journey itself becomes inseparable part of the reward.

It is primarily because of adventure that we read books and watch movies. Our imagination is captured by the unstoppable desire of finding out what will happen next in the story. Books will always hold a unique place as doors into parallel worlds, because they allow us to subconsciously slow down our reading speed in the middle of a scene to capture a particularly thrilling moment. In our mind, time literally slows down in the torrent of detailed descriptions as our reading speed slows to a crawl. Cinematographers have attempted to capture this effect on video using camera tricks, but it is only a bleak shadow of what the books can offer.

Virtual worlds also have a feature that is difficult to replicate. Interactivity allows us to insert ourselves into the story. We literally become inseparable part of the adventure, rather than simply observing it. The closest parallel to interactivity is live acting in theater or going on an actual real adventure in the wilderness, but in both of those cases you can be fairly certain of what to expect. Computer games strip typical expectations and take us on a journey that is exciting in new and unique ways. The power of the virtual world to convince you is called immersion. It lures the player into willful suspense of unbelief and liberates imagination.

How can a fake thrill be beneficial? Adventure is beneficial, because it transforms our character. For the same main reason why books and movies are beneficial, computer games also have a great potential to be beneficial. Virtual worlds immerse the player with an investment of freedom, which becomes soil for transformation. The player changes the virtual world by interacting with it, but in reality it is the player who is changed. The virtual world disappears when the computer is turned off, but the player stays changed. The degree of change increases over time as virtual worlds become more sophisticated. There are several studies which indicate a correlation between participation in virtual worlds and development of creativity among children.

Community

Computer games as a hobby do not necessarily make a person unsociable. In nations where almost every person has access to a computer, those who never visit virtual worlds are more likely to be missing out on social interactions. Games that are played the most and sell the most are overwhelmingly multiplayer games. There is a massive online network around each successful game with forums, Youtube channels, dedicated websites, blogs, and competition leagues. The size of a typical book club, chess club, sports team or a martial arts club, for instance, is half the size of the smallest virtual gaming communities.

Increasing levels of complexity in games demand persistent and reliable methods of communication, especially on a competitive level. With a growing number of games that require teamwork for success, gaming communities routinely utilize forums and voice chat for both socializing and playing. Groups that form around those information exchange hubs are commonly known as "guilds" or "clans." They are very common, tribal in structure, and tend to foster an environment for developing strong friendships.

Games designed for one player promote player interaction through scoreboards, strategy sharing, and "modding." Amateur programmers and artists build "mods" to change the games they enjoy. They add game content or change some of the game rules with a spirit of fan innovation, creativity, and humor. The closest analogy to a "mod" is a cover of a famous song by a rookie college band. Like songs, occasionally, the "mods" can become even more famous than the original games that they altered. A separate "modding community" forms around the most popular games.

There are many other opportunities to make new friends and to socialize, including conferences, fan clubs, competition leagues, and network parties. You may fear that friends made in online interactions are bound to be violent extremists or pedophiles, but by statistical odds this risk is currently rather small compared to normal daily human interactions. Communities built around gaming are usually fairly stable, open, and safe and provide a wonderful social benefit. Always investigate even if you have minor suspicions or form your own community with people you trust.

Sport

The fastest growing sport in the industrialized world is undeniably competitive Internet gaming. The exact rate of growth is hard to estimate, but the number of online chess and poker leagues and the number of participants in them has long passed their physical counterparts. The number of professional gamers is also growing rapidly, especially in South Korea. Game developers invest money into online leagues to promote the sales of their games. Computer hardware manufactures generously pitch in as well.

There is a reason for growing investment by big companies. In 2010, computer games in USA alone as an industry passed 25 billion USD mark. By comparison, that is more than the revenue from all professional American football, basketball, and baseball ticket sales combined! Classic sports still dominate television, but we really should be wondering for how long. Follow the money to see the future, and occasionally check Youtube to confirm the trends. We are entering the age of online sports.

We should not fear the demise of physical sport. Health benefits and enjoyment of rigorous physical training and competition cannot be matched by virtual activity. Sports in virtual worlds will not grow by detracting from classic sports but by developing a new market. In many cases, online entertainment may help promote physical sports. Great examples of that include American "Fantasy Football" and games based on active sports and dance.

Spiritual and social benefits of sport are commonly found in virtual worlds to an ever increasing degree. Competition builds personal confidence and a sense of mutual respect between players. It teaches how to learn to accept failure and grow from it through adaptation and practice. It promotes learning and social interaction. In fact, there is not a single computer game world champion who earned his title without a help of a team of training partners. All the work that is required to earn the title through reliance on information acquired from others produces proper attitude of sportsmanship and humility that is often lacking in professional athletes. In this sense, games can occasionally have an even greater potential for training virtue in soul through competition than even physical sport.

Learning

Computer games teach effectively, and some things are learned in a virtual world better than by other means. The first ones to realize this were the airline companies and the military. Mechanical flight simulators were first used even before World War I. Today, training by means of virtual flight simulators is the industry standard. Several generations of both civilian and military pilots were trained in virtual reality to a significant degree before they were allowed to fly a real plane or helicopter. Virtual training is now invading the medical world, and the US military developed their own computer games for teaching basic combat tactics.

Cost has a lot to do with the advent of virtual reality in educational fields. Military and medical mistakes can be rather costly. Making those mistakes in a virtual world costs nothing. The better the virtual world reflects the reality, the better is the quality of the training, and the lower is the cost of training. Technology will continue to revolutionize education by means of virtual worlds, especially in chemistry and engineering.

Advanced learning software can be rather expensive, but regular computer games often provide learning benefits. When I was in college, I played "Total War" series extensively, which is a collection of games that let you run an ancient empire and fight great realistic battles in vast military campaigns. In the game, I was a leader of Carthaginian Empire and my main enemies were Romans. By battling Romans for 300 years in the game, I learned the entire map of ancient Mediterranean, including every major ancient city and geographical feature of every province. There is not a teacher on earth who could force this information down my throat by any other means. Geography is atrocious enemy of human race! Or so I thought before I started working on my thesis in graduate school. I wish I got the memo sooner: history is meaningless without the study of geography. I seldom read a history book now that does not reference an area around the Mediterranean Sea, and most of the time I know exactly what place the historian is talking about because of the games I used to play.

I was not the only one to notice the didactic potential of "Total War" games. History Channel started using them to stage historic battles for television audiences. This is just one example of many that could be cited. As computer game industry grows and develops, the educational value of each world also increases. Recently, in fact, Rice University offered a course in Nordic and Icelandic mythology and its influence on modern literature and art. The central piece of curriculum for this college class was "Skyrim," a popular fantasy role playing game about slaying dragons. I am sure the class was over-packed with male students, and they probably learned a lot more than students typically learn in a literature class.

Art

I am deeply convinced that computer games are the highest form of art, and that they will become a dominant art form soon. The main reason for this conviction is the simple observation that every other form of art can be included inside a virtual world. Paintings, cinema, theater, fiction, architecture, interior design, drama, sculpture, and music – you name it – all those things are routinely found in virtual worlds in many different combinations. On top of that, all those art forms are expanded through interactivity and enhanced through immersion. They become part of the living and breathing virtual world.

It may sounds surprising to you, but the computer game industry already employs more artists than any other. In fact, the vast majority of development teams are basically artists. So if you are thinking about a career in art for yourself or your child, you may have to start thinking about computer games. To produce even a low-budget computer game, a company has to hire a professional writer, an art director, several graphic artists, a music producer, a sound engineer, and a character designer. The most valuable parts of the finished game are usually the art assets created for it, because they make the game identifiably unique and marketable. A growing number of modern games are created by simply providing new art for a licensed third-party game engines. This trend will continue cementing the undeniable reality that computer game industry is the world's leading art market.

Art is to be enjoyed for its own sake. That is why we call some things "art" so arbitrarily. The "artful things" are just there for us to examine and ponder their deeper meaning. The exact benefits of art are even more difficult to outline than the definition of art itself. Something about it causes us to stop and think, and those thoughts can profoundly affect us. And if paintings by Picasso still count for beneficial art because of the impression they make on the observer, computer games can be top-shelf art.

Inexpensive Leisure

Computer games have become the cheapest popular form of entertainment, especially if you stay away from gaming consoles like Play Station and XBox. If you wanted to play the best games before 2010, you had to invest a lot of money into an expensive specialized gaming computer. Today, the average laptop for college students can handle almost all games on reduced settings with few exceptions. Games used to hold their value steadily for several years. Now, most games on PC can be purchased for half their initial value within six months after the release date. This is a result of the increased market competition between studios and the demise of physical retail game stores.

Most games are bought on the Internet and downloaded directly to the computer or a mobile device. There are several major online stores that compete for customers with each other and with software pirates. They lower the prices to stay in business. Stores save a lot of money by not having to ship product physically, and they pass the savings back to the customer. Holiday sales in online stores can provide limitless high quality entertainment at the cost of about ten cents per hour when you purchase bundles of games. The fact that many old and classic games can be better than most new games makes those purchases quite a bargain.

The volume of entertainment value is also staggering. In our town, going out to a movie or a restaurant costs roughly two or three hours of minimum wage. For the same money, you can easily get fifty to one hundred hours of high quality game time from one of the online stores. I cannot think of anything that I have ever done for fun that has been this cheap, even when I was growing up in communist Russia. If you already own a computer, reading books is at the very least five times more expensive than playing computer games!

CHAPTER 3

DANGERS OF VIRTUAL WORLDS

"I signed up for Second Life about a year ago. Back then, my life was so great I literally wanted a second one. Absolutely everything was the same... except I could fly." – Dwight Schrute, The Office

Virtual worlds are dangerous. Players enjoy immense freedom in them proportionately to the size of the game. Freedom generates an exhilarating sense of discovery and adventure, but it has real potential to hurt the persons involved in exercising this freedom. The existence of this potential by itself should not deter us from entering the virtual world. This same potential exists in every area of our lives. What should concern us is nature and extent of the consequences that follow prolonged exposure.

We may never feel a desire to murder or steal just out of curiosity, but we may hesitate little to try those things in a virtual world. After all, if the virtual police arrest you in the game, you can just restart the game with a clean slate and numbed conscience. There are no permanent criminal records or deaths in virtual worlds. There is no true authority to judge players or oppose them. The subject of freedom and ethics in computer games deserves a separate book. For our purposes, we should simply acknowledge a real presence of danger in virtual worlds that comes with freedom offered in them. One cannot exist without the other.

Perceived Dangers

The mere possibility of danger has been a source of senseless fear of virtual worlds for many years. There has seldom been a case of teenage brutality that was not blamed on computer games by the media. School shootings are especially hard to deal with. Waves of lawsuits and finger pointing follow each one driven by the desire to make sense of what transpired. Computer games make a handy scape goat, if God himself is not blamed and sued for damages. Violence in computer games is generally an overstated concern, although there are exceptions like the infamous Grand Theft Auto series.

Teenage involvement in violent computer games is more likely a reflection of our violent culture rather than a direct cause of brutality. The vast majority of teenagers in industrial nations play violent computer games, especially boys. The myth that those games are the primary cause of violence perpetuates because the public is uninformed. As a result, much of parental and public concern is misdirected. There are real dangers in virtual worlds, but most of the effort is wasted on opposing perceived dangers. We will discuss both sets of dangers to better understand what we are dealing with, so that in the next chapter we can learn to effectively remedy the primary ills of gaming.

Violent Behavior

Criticism of computer games for violent content is strange, in the face of prevalent grotesque violence in other forms of media. Once I attended a party hosted by a family from our church, and a group of about twenty children of different ages were put in a separate room to watch a movie while the adults enjoyed the things that they do in such social gatherings. My curiosity sprung by loud uncontrollable laughter coming from the room full of kids. I peeked into the room. They were watching one of those movies about Dalmatian puppies. Most of them were rolling on the floor pointing with hilarity at the screen. What was happening on the screen? A villain was unsuccessfully trying to get into a building by taking stairs. What was so funny about it? He was falling on the stairs continuously and hurting himself.

The spectacle really got me thinking. The scene was rather long and detailed with camera zooming in on places where the villain was hurt the most. It instantly summoned memories of thousands of similar scenes in iconic family movies like "Home Alone" and classic cartoons like "Tom and Jerry." Violence must be immensely entertaining! Then, I realized that it was tough to recall any popular movie or book that was devoid of violence. The most famous scene in "Star Wars" involves a gruesome amputation of Luke's limb by his own father. Among the best-selling books, the Bible is one of the most graphic and violent.

Observing violence in a story seems to be an important part of the plot. What happens when you are in the story as a participant in the plot? In one recent game, you are expected to execute hostages as a part of infiltrating a terrorist organization. Later in the game, this organization is destroyed as a consequence of your infiltration. Did the ends justify the means and legitimize the first atrocity committed by the player? Violence is often an ornament to the difficult and profound choices that players have to make in games.

If there is a problem with violence in virtual worlds, the problem is seldom with the presence of violence but with the kind of violence that is found in them. Virtual worlds tend to cheapen and trivialize violence and divorce it from real hurt. It is psychologically difficult to inflict pain on somebody else. Professional torturers are trained for their craft. Professional criminals grow in violence through practice. Computer games instill repetitious violence that does not really have an entry barrier, because the consequences of inflicting pain on an agent and the reaction of the agent are sanitized. Pain becomes devoid of meaning.

Although this is a real danger, it is currently less acute problem than violence in movies and books. Successful games are marketed internationally. They are easy to export worldwide and companies prefer to reach the widest audiences possible to make the most money. Since the laws vary between nations, companies generally cater to stricter laws in countries like Australia to secure mass appeal of their product and ensure the largest possible audience. Since teenage males represent a hefty chunk of the market, most companies reach for that precious "Teenage" rating which is hard to maintain worldwide without curbing the gore. The end result is that successful computer games are far less violent and pornographic on average than successful books and movies bar a few notorious exceptions. Virtual worlds are also given much better age restrictions than either books or movies for that same reason.

Social Isolation

Computer games are often credited with degrading the attention spans of the young and isolating them from their peers. Many social benefits of virtual worlds were presented in the previous chapter. Abundance of opportunities to make friends does not guarantee that each player will turn into a social butterfly. It is common to be surrounded by people from all sides and feel desperately alone.

Technology is making the world a smaller place, but it is also changing the way we develop relationships. We have a lot more friends than our ancestors, but the quality and depth of those friendships is rightly questioned.

Computer games are easy to blame for the growing decline of meaningful relationships, especially since a disproportionate amount of time is allotted to virtual exploration by teenagers. While virtual worlds may contribute to this decline, the growing share of time devoted to computer games is more likely to be a symptom of other alarming social patterns than a direct cause of isolation. In industrial nations, parents spend a lot less time interacting with their children than ever before.

Relationships between parents and children are of key importance, because they set the pattern for all other relationships that children will have in their life. Levels of parental involvement in upbringing and education of their children dictate future academic success more than giftedness. Children struggle to develop close friendships, if they do not have a concept of close friendship in their mind that they learned from people close to them. They have a tough time getting to know other people, if people they live with have tried little to get to know them. The angst of loneliness is often at the heart of substance abuse, eating disorders, masochism, and suicide.

A person absorbed by a virtual world is most likely self-medicating without realizing it. They find a safe haven and solace in fantasy. An interesting study conducted by East Carolina University titled "The Effectiveness of Casual Video Games in Improving Mood and Decreasing Stress" claims that computer games can sometimes be more effective in treating clinical depression and anxiety disorders than medicine. All of this is said not to push blame on the parents, who can be just as lonely and socially dysfunctional as the children that they are trying to help. Rather, this is said to help us diagnose our problems so that we do not cripple each other further with simplistic and misguided solutions.

Virtual worlds provide a rich environment in which it is easy to acquire common memories and experiences. Having something in common helps us make new friends, and most friendships are formed around shared interests. Modern folklore is built around stories from computer games. Geekiness has now become hipster and cool, and simply knowing what "Fus-Roh-Dah" means can make you a lot of new friends. "Fus-Roh-Dah" is a magical battle cry from the game "Skyrim" that knocks your foes down from their feet. It has inspired hundreds of mock videos and jokes and has become a vital part of the Internet culture. This is a classic example of a powerful domination of the Internet culture by folklore coming out of computer games.

Cultural trends draw the barriers between people that direct the structure of social circles. While playing games has been a hobby of select few in the past, now adventures in virtual worlds are mainstream. Since there is always a set of games that virtually every person who plays regularly is familiar with, learning a little bit about recently successful or classic games can help you build an instant connection with another person even from the other side of the world. Familiarity with those games is probably the single most significant thing you might have in common! I helped a college student move to our town in 2013. He grew up in India, and I grew up in Russia. How much do you think two young men from cultures so different and so distant might have in common? In this day and age, a lot. We instantly connected over our interest in heavy metal music and computer games. We had hours of things to talk about, even though we had just met. Healthy excursions into virtual worlds will not put you in social isolation, they will bring you into cultural solidarity with this generation globally.

Intellectual Stagnation

Virtual worlds are frequently charged with dulling the minds of young people and stunting their intellectual development. The core cause of this concern is the positive reinforcement loop that is sometimes sustained during the gaming process. The game continuously praises and awards the player for accomplishments that do not exist. Positive reinforcement loop is a repetitive reward cycle intended to keep the person continuously involved in a virtual activity. Each virtual achievement is followed by a grandiose celebration. The player is praised for his or her success and given another challenge to strive for. Since those virtual rewards have little value outside of the virtual world, the entire process is perceived as mind-numbing. The brain is thought to go into passive cathartic state, lulled into gradual degenerative atrophy.

This process may occasionally entrap a person in certain kinds of games which are designed to exploit the player. We will discuss how to recognize those games in the following chapter. Generally speaking, however, few activities can stimulate the brain more than adventures in virtual worlds. In most cases, the opposite is true: virtual worlds provide some of the best ways of developing intelligence. That includes various kinds of intelligence. Academic performance can be boosted with educational games. Problem solving is developed with puzzle-driven games. Common sense and street wisdom are taught by the narratives of crime and police dramas. Social intelligence develops over time in multiplayer games. In fact, the levels of neural stimulation are so intense that they often become the most powerful cause of gaming addiction. Human mind really likes to be challenged. Our lives can be seen as positive reinforcement loops of the treadmill we call career. If the statistics are right, our careers are rewarding and worthwhile only half the time. No wonder that the virtual challenge often brings more excitement!

Neural stimulation is intensified even more in competitive multiplayer setting, which leads to continual development of the intellect. It is impossible to compete without naturally improving over time at least in some aspects of the intellect. StarCraft has become South Korean national sport. It is a rather complicated real-time version of chess, in which the players try to eliminate each other by moving their pieces at the same time. A typical match lasts about twenty minutes, during which professional StarCraft players perform an average of over 200 actions per minute. During the most intense parts of the game, when player armies collide in battle, they peak at 300-450 actions per minute. Each action is a key stroke or a mouse click. This means that each player will execute over 200,000 commands in one game in order to overcome their opponent. Do you know any other activity, besides piloting a helicopter through a thunderstorm, which would require you to make over 200,000 calculated decisions in twenty minutes?

It is hard to find a competitive chess player who ranks poorly in intellectual feats. It is even harder to find a competitive computer gamer who does not pass the population average in intellectual ability by a significant margin. Intellect is tricky to measure and evaluate. God gives us smarts and capacity for developing wits. Every person has an immense ability to improve their intelligence, and virtual worlds are the best known incubators for that purpose. And even though each game is different in its effects, virtual worlds as a whole do not stunt intellectual development but promote it.

One of the top private schools in the Silicon Valley does not allow or use any electronic devices for students at all. Another school nearby heavily promotes learning by using electronic education and encourages the use of computer games in classes for learning. Both schools produce excellent students and compete well with each other, but the second one does it at much lower cost. Teachers are now starting to use virtual worlds to teach some of their curriculum and report a great degree of success in test performance and student participation. Since the cost of educational software is becoming astronomically low compared to other forms of education, the teaching profession may soon disappear. Or we should rather say, professional teachers will all soon become professional tutors assisting, configuring, and servicing the educational virtual software remotely. As those early trends are steadily turning into universal reality, the fact that virtual worlds are some of the powerful stimulants of our intellect becomes undeniable.

Real Dangers

While violent behavior, social isolation, and intellectual stagnation are commonly associated with computer games, those things are overall a relatively minor source of risk for most people unless they have a prior history of dealing with those issues. It does not mean that those concerns should be taken lightly, but that they should not overshadow in importance far greater dangers that accompany virtual worlds listed below. Focus your energy on dealing with greater dangers first and be also mindful of minor things in proportion to their weight. So what are the greatest dangers of virtual worlds?

Addictiveness

Addictiveness of virtual worlds is a hotly debated subject. Actual addiction rates seem rather low among both children and adults who play computer games regularly. Physical symptoms of addiction are also relatively insignificant compared to other common forms of addiction. In worst cases, addicts develop headaches, irritability, and eye strain. Nonetheless, social consequences of compulsive gaming can be devastating. For that reason, addiction to computer games is sometimes classified as a psychological disease, and there are centers that offer treatment for this addiction.

Medical community disagrees on everything that has to do with virtual world and addictiveness, and a consensus is nowhere in sight. The reason why medical community is having so much trouble producing reliable data is their historic undiscerning selection of games for trials, although this is beginning to change somewhat. Some games are far more addictive than others. Ironically, the most addictive games of all are those that provide the most opportunities for social interaction between players. Some games are purposefully designed to be addictive. Companies, like Blizzard Entertainment, spend literally an extra year of time and extra millions of dollars on each of their games, after they already finished creating it, just to make sure that they are irresistible and addictive to the largest number of people possible. Of course, they target the young and impressionable customers the most.

There are several game companies that have a reputation in the Internet community for exploiting the virtual world market. Those companies achieve great monetary success by making addictive and repetitive games. If they figure out a good way to hypnotize players, they will keep releasing the same game over and over again with slightly updated graphics. They are backed by major investors with powerful marketing tools. Movie contracts and merchandize rain from the sky in their wake. This is already becoming a fertile ground for conspiracy theorists and script writers to prophesy the coming age of new slavery, where people will exchange their real things for fake things in virtual worlds with glee.

Examples of odd online auction sales associated with addictive games abound, some of which surpass a quarter of a million dollars in final price. That is right – some people pay that much money to acquire an asset that, technically, is purely imaginary. The use of game mechanics for behavior modification is called "gamification." In Soviet Union, Vladimir Lenin was trying to figure out ways to increase the productivity of the working class without increasing their wages. He ended up creating competitions between factories. Each factory formed a team that competed in productivity against factories next to it. The winning teams received badges and medals in elaborate mandatory award ceremonies. He created many tiers of competitions and with many different kinds of rewards. For each level you complete, you get a reward. Does that begin to sound familiar? For your real effort, you get a virtual reward. This system of gamification is at the core of every religious cult, and it is also a prevalent part of many virtual worlds.

Sometimes the market conditions created by gamification result in pure evil. Virtual gold sales in top online multiplayer game World of Warcraft have become infamous. In one example, a Chinese prison warden forced all his prisoners to play this game for 12 hours a day in continuous shifts. All the virtual gold collected this way was sold on the black market, and the proceeds were used to pay bribes to keep this secret and to provide a huge salary to the warden. There are some estimates claiming that there are at least 100,000 virtual gold farmers turning over two billion dollars in cash yearly in China alone, and a significant percentage of those are indentured by debt or other means.

Addictiveness of computer games is growing and developing into new forms, even monetary forms. Risk is foundational to the appeal of the virtual worlds. They promise satisfaction and reward to venturesome players. The continual pursuit of reward can be exhilarating, and cause harmful behaviors similar to destructive behaviors that are sometimes associated with gambling. Playing for money is not gambling in itself. There are many professional poker players that compete in poker as sport by becoming the best at calculating mathematical probabilities, applying psychology, and social intuition. Making bets can be an extension of expertise and cold calculation. Gambling has more to do with inner impulses than the presence or absence of cash in the game. Playing turns into gambling the moment the person begins to enjoy the thrill of risk and becomes consumed by the greed coming from their irresistible desire to attain the expected reward. Gambling is a serious and devastating addiction, because it drives people to take risks that they absolutely cannot afford to take. Even while losing everything, the player enjoys the process for the faint hope of large winnings. Once this addiction controls the player, they are eventually destroyed by unmanageable debt. And, people who are closest to the gambler are hurt the most. The presence of risk in computer games can mimic the effects of a real gambling addiction.

Since the reward itself is usually virtual and not physical, the symptoms and consequences of a gambling addiction developed in a virtual world tend to keep mild compared to those caused by a real gambling addiction. Players may be compelled to spend exuberant amounts of money on virtual goods to feed their addiction, but it will rarely cause them to be indebted to criminal loan sharks. It is a sure bet, however, that in the near future virtual worlds will become the primary source of devastating gambling addiction as games become more commercial and commonplace. For this reason, everybody must be aware of the real danger of developing a complex powerful addiction in the virtual world that shares traits and severity of many other known forms of addictions including gambling.

Time Dilation

Change marks the passing of time. The magnitude and types of changes we experience determine our perception of time. Big changes give us the impression that a lot of time has passed. Small changes can make us think that time has stopped. Virtual worlds can manipulate time in interesting and unusual ways. Games can be fast paced or easy going. Time can turn and change in the middle of the playing process. Almost all games allow players to reverse the flow of time by letting them save their progress and load it back. If you play a computer game for thirty minutes and lose, you may load the game from the last saved file and replay the same thirty minutes all over again. At this point, you have spent one hour on the game, but your senses are fooled. Since your brain is accustomed to measuring time by the degree of perceived change, you will actually feel as if you have been in the game for only half of that time.

Even though it may seem that there are many things happening at once on the screen, the actual total amount of change is much smaller than the amount of change we are accustomed to experiencing daily in the physical world. A typical completely boring day at work brings about many new things. We filter out and forget everything except the most important parts of what happened in order to stay sane. But the changes that were detected by our brains and discarded as unessential were essential for our senses for demarcating time. The rustling of the leaves, the insect the on bathroom wall, the postman passing by, the car accident on the commute are things happening all around us. Tiny insignificant things that we do not think we notice are actually absorbed subconsciously for later processing. Since things in virtual worlds change much less than real things, our brains are duped and lose track of time.

As far as our perceptions are concerned, things are going slow when we navigate the virtual world, really slow. That is why it is so easy to get completely absorbed in the game while you play. We experience something similar in our dreams, in which normally just a few people talk to us and a few minor things change. If we wake up while having a dream, it is difficult to tell what time it is the moment that you woke up. If you are interrupted while enjoying a good game, you will naturally look at your watch. Checking what time it is after playing a game is a funny quirk that most people who play a lot will eventually develop. After leaving the virtual world, we look for a way to fall back into the normal flow of routine.

Most are unaware of this effect until it manifests itself in patterns of destructive escapism. There are studies that show correlations between poor health, especially obesity, and long gaming hours. Every year several infants die because of parental neglect or violence in connection with poor gaming habits. In one iconic case in South Korea, a girl died of starvation while her parents were raising a virtual baby. According to some estimates, 15% of wives have reported that they feel that their husbands care more about computer games than about them. In other words, virtual escapism will be the primary cause of divorce in at least 15% of the cases in this generation. Because of virtual time dilation, husbands are not realizing that they are spending a lot more time in the virtual worlds than with their families. The total amount of observable change by which they measure time seems the same to them.

It is important to understand that the root cause is not the intention of the addict to avoid their daily responsibilities and commitments, but their inability to recognize that their senses have become paralyzed by the effects of virtual time dilation. One of the best ways of dealing with this is to make mandatory short breaks every half an hour or so during the gaming session. Leaving the virtual world even briefly and stepping away from the computer helps the brain resynchronize with the normal flow of time and gain traction with the physical. And it is a lot easier to convince somebody to take regular breaks than to convince them to reduce their total playing hours. In fact, if they start taking regular breaks, they will end up playing less overall. We will discuss this further in the following section.

Radical Dualism

Dualism is the idea that everything in life can be thought of as belonging to only one of two broad possible categories. This belief first appears in early classic philosophy and regularly emerges in different ways in culture, academics, and politics. Dividing things into two groups is a convenient way of manipulating people by offering them only two choices, when in reality more possibilities exist. Movies commonly employ dualism as a plot device by unraveling a conflict between light and darkness. The "good guys" always win, and the "bad guys" always lose. The "good guys" are always right, and the "bad guys" are always wrong.

In the first chapter, we briefly discussed that monsters in computer games are often portrayals of human sins and vices. Slaying those monsters as an allegory for overcoming our sins and temptations can be understood as a spiritual journey. In many modern games, however, the monsters are presented as human characters. They have human shells, but they behave like a horde of mindless monsters. This effect can simply be a result of inherent limitations of game design. It is difficult to mimic intelligence and personality, especially the human kinds of intelligence and personality. As a result, human enemies are effectively dehumanized. They do not have a lick of common sense. They charge straight into danger like zombies, they do not communicate meaningfully with the players or with each other, and they do not understand any reason or compromise.

Hordes of flat human-like characters in virtual worlds objectify and dehumanize a class of people that they represent and make them appear like monsters. Virtual worlds are currently the single most active and potent force of promoting racist propaganda. Some extreme examples include games that simulate Holocaust by letting players run their own concentration camps and profit from selling teeth feelings, shoes, and soap. More common are racist portrayals of Arabs, Chinese, Russians, and Germans as the "enemy horde." Certain groups are routinely made into punching dummies by game developers. Movies have a typical line up of villain races as well, but games take it a step further because the player leads the banishment of the other group that is considered evil.

Our culture, being sensitive to racism, has also produced some comical situations in virtual worlds by trying to avoid being racist. In many games now there is an opportunity to pick a character from most racial groups, but those characters by their very presentation often deepen and exacerbate racial stereotypes rather than help alleviate them. Women are also objectified in similar ways. They are commonly presented as rewards or decorations with exaggerated features common to the gender. This is especially true of female villains – it is hard to find a homely one, because the narrative makes them into objects of conquest.

By "radical dualism" in virtual worlds I mean to say that this division of everything into two groups is exaggerated. Full extent of this effect will not be felt until the next generation, when almost every young person would have been programmed from infancy to think of people in just two categories. This type of thinking promotes bullying, because having fun at another person's expense is considered permissible as long as the person in question is being thought as being part of the outsiders. Scams and theft are commonplace in multiplayer virtual worlds, and most of those are not motivated by the desire to attain the object being stolen but by the desire to inflict suffering on the person from which the object is stolen.

Cyberbalkanization

Radical dualism of the virtual worlds compounds the negative effects of cyberbalkanization. Balkanization is a process of continual separation into groups that are growing in hostility toward each other. Historically, this term has been used to describe the decay of larger countries when they fall apart into small semi-autonomous states with bitterness and even hatred between each other. Balkanization is not merely a political process. It is mainly a social phenomenon describing behavior and attitudes of people in mixed groups as they break up into homogenous groups. It commonly results in wars with fragmentation along the lines of race, culture, and economic status. In fact, the term comes from the violent conflicts that took place on the Balkan Peninsula in Europe between different cultural groups. The degree of brutality, recklessness, and hatred in those conflicts shocked the world in light of the fact that the people killing each other so ruthlessly had lived so closely together for many years and had so much in common.

Cyberbalkanization is a similar phenomenon describing the degradation of persons involved in Internet communities. It is a natural process fueled by normal human tendencies. In certain circumstances, it is unavoidable. If left unchecked, it becomes detrimental for everyone involved. It is especially dangerous because the people who are controlled by it the most are usually the least aware of it.

It starts with friendships. We love to make friends, and we prefer to make friends with people who have something in common with us. Everybody is different, but there are always some things that are in common. It takes less effort to make friends with people who have a lot in common with us. The Internet's greatest danger is the ease with which it connects us to people who are almost exactly like us. For example, you may be able to find just three or four friends who share most of your hobbies and interests among all the people that you have physically met. On the Internet, you can find several thousand people who share all your hobbies and interests within minutes.

If you connect with this group, you may feel like you found heaven. Finally, somebody understands how you feel and accepts you as you are! The more this group socializes with itself and with you, the more pickled everyone becomes in their own juice. Sameness is mistaken for intimacy and loyalty. In reality, the great love you are experiencing is the fascination with self in a mirror of people who are just like you. You are no longer interested in other people but in enjoying your own personality traits reflected from them.

There are millions of groups plagued by cyberbalkanization on the Internet. The main culprits are political and religious communities, but there is really no group that is completely immune to this process. Pick any hobby or interest and look for top Internet forums associated with it. You will often find roughly ten to twenty people at the heart of it, and you may think they are insanely obsessed with their interest. But within this group, all the members think of each other as normal and consider those outside of the group weird.

The existence of a cultural bubble is not damaging by itself. Chronic problems blossom later, when the members begin to spend the majority of their life in that cultural bubble. They become suspicious and critical of the outsiders. They naturally expel newcomers unless they fit a certain set of unspoken expectations. They begin to think of themselves as heroes making a stand against imaginary external oppressors. Virtual worlds are a fertile soil to grow mutant cyberbalkanized narrow-minded communities around. They create an outlet for sinking time into a common interest that creates human social clones.

How can you tell if cyberbalkanization is starting to take over a community group? Check if the group is losing diversity. How many different races, ages, cultures, professions and educational backgrounds are represented in the group? Check if the group has its own special way of speaking. Large quantities of technical language, foul words, and repetitive phrases is a dead give away of a community wrapped up in itself. Do they use unusual amounts of strange terminology and inside jokes, so that an outsider would feel completely lost or uncomfortable? Check if the group is remaining static for long periods of time. Are there any regular changes to the activities and structure of the group? Do new people want to join this group? Are activities of this group perceived as more important than what happens outside of this group?

The risk of cyberbalkanization by itself is not a good reason to avoid all gaming communities. To some extent, this process is unavoidable in any social setting. This warning against it is not intended to motivate you to completely avoid it, lest you never leave your house for the rest of your life, but to motivate you to learn to recognize it and manage its negative effects. Most churches are plagued by similar negative social trends with active hostility toward outsiders. That does not constitute a good reason to avoid church, but it does call us to actively oppose those trends in order to improve our community. In the following chapter, we will ponder some constructive ways of reversing those and other negative trends discussed previously.

CHAPTER 4

PSYCHOLOGICAL SELF-DEFENSE

"I cannot keep a bird from flying over my head. But I can certainly keep it from nesting in my hair or from biting my nose off." – Martin Luther

The presence of danger is not a sufficient reason by itself to justify entirely avoiding virtual worlds. With the rapid growth of mobile technology, it is virtually impossible to shield yourself and your family from virtual interactions. Even though we cannot avoid virtual interactions, we can always do something to guard ourselves and others from dangers associated with them. If we understand what we are dealing with and how to respond to it, we can find safety in the shelter of informed responsibility. Psychological self-defense is a discipline and a skill developed over time. Our ability to make correct decisions in virtual worlds is a test of character. We cannot ignore or downplay threats we face, but we can learn to respond correctly to dangerous situations through moral character training.

Everybody takes precautions to protect their family from physical dangers. We also think of ways to get out of dangerous situations ahead of time and develop habits that would reduce the risks of a physical attack. I always tell my wife to have car keys in her hand before she gets to the car door when she walks through a parking lot, because I know that parking lots are a common place where women can be attacked. The chance that my family will suffer a physical attack is small. But since the consequences of such an attack could be devastating, I take every possible precaution to keep my family safe. We are practicing self-defense.

Even though the virtual worlds are imaginary, thinking that reality and virtual reality are completely disconnected is dangerous. What goes on in our head affects everything that we do in most significant ways. Our thoughts lay rail-road tracks for our actions. They tug at our convictions in different directions and disrupt our sensibilities. We must practice psychological self-defense in order to be aware of those dangers. Even though the overall risk of getting into a bad situation is small, the compounded effect of multiple bad situations that you allow yourself into can destroy your life. Below are some basic strategies that will help you and your family stay out of trouble.

Practice Selectivity

Marketing geniuses identified a unique compulsion that most people develop in a game they might greatly enjoy. This compulsion is our desire to do everything that is possible to do in that virtual world in order to attain a sense of accomplishment or for bragging rights. We desire to feel as if we did not miss any opportunities in that particular game because we liked it. Many companies exploit this desire mercilessly by adding "achievement badges" to games that reward you for completing trivial, repetitive, and strange tasks. For example, if you collect one thousand additional coins above what might normally be required, you will get an achievement badge rewarding your great diligence. If it takes twenty hours to beat the game, it might take another sixty additional hours to earn the extra achievements. It may take even more time to get to 100% game completion, when all the "achievement badges" were unlocked and collected. If a game aggressively promotes "achievement rewards," it is probably a good sign that it is better to throw this game away. It is undermining your first line of psychological self-defense: selectivity.

We cannot always choose dangers in the real world, but we can choose dangers we encounter in the virtual worlds. We can even choose which virtual worlds we visit, and there is always an option to turn the game off. Do not let marketing tricks cloud your judgment. There is nothing in any virtual world that must be taken to final completion! If the game makes you feel uncomfortable, turn it off. If it becomes boring or repetitive, turn it off. If you can no longer see any profit in it, turn it off. There are many other things you could do, and many other games you could play.

Never feel obligated to play each game to the end to beat it entirely. It is best not to. Most games are really not worth your time, so being selective is not only wise but necessary. If you find it frustrating, boring, repetitive, or morally questionable for yourself or your family, discard it. There is another game that could be played or another activity that could be enjoyed. Do not try to beat every game on the toughest difficulty level either. As a general rule, play games on easy mode to save time. If you feel compelled to complete everything to 100%, you may be exhibiting signs of addiction.

It is difficult to instill restraint and selectivity in children, because they want to play all the games that their friends play, even though their friends might be playing different sets of games. You can use the fact that kids play a lot of different kinds of games to your advantage. If your children are begging you to get a certain game, ask them to tell you the names of the most popular games that their friends play. They may be more agreeable when you present them with alternatives of your choosing from that list. By doing this, you are also teaching your children how to be selective and which principles to employ when making a mature and wise decisions. Those principles may stay with them long after they grow up.

Computer game market is booming. There is a massive variety of games on the market, which makes it easy to apply selectivity. If you like one particular game but find some aspects of it that make you uncomfortable, there are usually four to five other games similar to it. If the game seems too violent or crude, it will not be difficult to find another game that is far less objectionable of the same kind. Shop around. Most popular games have free trial versions, trailers, and reviews. You can also easily find an online video stream of another person playing that game, which will help you make the decision.

What factors should influence your decision? Definitely look at ESRB ratings (www.esrb.org) first. This organization does a much better job than similar ones that rate movies and TV content. Second, read some reviews to get familiar with the game plot and basic gameplay. The storyline is the most important part of the game, because there are no stories that are amoral. Every story teaches something about good and evil, and many stories teach it the wrong way. Do not expose yourself to questionable moral subliminal instruction past your maturity level. Judge yourself about this and ask others for their best honest input. Keep in mind that in those games you will often be a participant and not just an observer. Let me paraphrase the words of Jesus Christ: if you have imagined doing something bad you are perceived by God just as guilty as if you have actually done it. That is a sobering statement and a stern warning!

There are games in which criminal activity is a part of character progression in the story and even part of that character's eventual redemption, just like there are many stories of redemption in all of literature and movies. Just make sure that you are mature enough to be able to tell the difference between a temporary moral lapse of a character for the sake of the story and a permanent moral collapse for the sake of glorifying evil. This line is often blurred, and, if you catch yourself unable to discern which way is up and which way is down in a given virtual world, you should look for another one to visit.

Practice selectivity by switching between games to help ease attachment to any one particular game. If you tend to play frequently, playing just one game all the time puts you at higher risk of addiction than switching between different kinds of games. Virtual worlds have varying degrees of addictiveness and varying durations of appeal. Switching it up will break some of the more dangerous reward cycles. You will also grow in your discernment faster, because you will have more reference points from which to make good decisions about your further adventures in virtual worlds.

Foster Discipline

Discipline is continual effort to developing healthy and profitable habits. Virtual worlds can be powerful and addictive distractions. They will challenge your sense of moderation. It is not uncommon to continue to play games in your head even after you have turned the computer off. This can negatively affect your job performance and your family relationships. There are also potential negative medical consequences like additional stress and anxiety, eye strain, hypertension, headache, and sleeplessness. You can overcome those risks by fostering discipline.

Start with your time management skills. Estimate the amount of time that each gaming session will take out of your day. You should stay away from any game that requires you to remain stationary for more than half of hour or games that do not have a pause button. Some games have built-in parental controls that block the game after a certain amount of time or demand a regular mandatory break. There are also inexpensive software packages that can enforce those rules in all your home computers. Even if you are a fully mature adult, there is no shame in restricting yourself with parental controls and giving the password for it to your spouse. This initial limitation which can be removed later will help you develop good playing habits right away, and it will make it easier for you to put restrictions on your children or siblings. If you submit to some additional disciple, even when you do not need it, you will give younger members of your household an example of obedience. Children, and in some cases grown-ups, need to understand that adulthood is not absence of discipline but stringent self-discipline and openness to accountability. There is no better way to teach this to others than to live it.

You can limit the amount of influence games have on you by denying them opportunities to dominate your thoughts. If you are easily drawn into virtual worlds, simply restricting yourself is seldom enough to maintain a healthy life style. A persistent and gnawing temptation will eventually burst into a binge. The greatest enemy of discipline is not laziness but boredom. Self-denial by itself produces limited positive effect and creates vacuous boredom unless there is something to replace what has been denied. Having multiple hobbies is not only helpful, but it is important for sanity. If you or a family member are having trouble with discipline, picking up a new hobby can help significantly. Sports and music are great standard candidates for hobbies, but anything that you enjoy doing or find interesting will do.

Your enjoyment level of many games can be actually increased if you develop a hobby in a related area. For instance, if you enjoy games that put you in charge of commanding armies, you may also enjoy reading historical novels and going to museums. If you like medieval fantasy games, picking up archery or javelin for sport will increase your appreciation for both. If you like fighting games, get into martial arts. Discipline learned through mastery of the physical sport will carry over into virtual settings or the rest of your life. Actually that is really the best advice I have. You can stop reading this book if you pick up a physical sport – I will not have anything else to teach you that your coach or trainer will not.

It is still a good idea to practice self-denial from time to time just for the sake of training your spirit. This ancient art is called fasting, and it has tremendous benefits for low costs in all areas of your life. From time to time, take a fast from technology and go completely off-grid. It is hard to do initially, but it will reconnect you with a true sense of freedom. Elephants in India are tied to wooden posts when they are young. They struggle at first to break free, but after a few years they quit trying and can be held in place by a thin thread as long as it is visibly attached to a wooden stake. You are smarter than an elephant – you can learn to break free.

Develop Community

Being part of a gaming community is mandatory for developing healthy gaming habits. When I lived in Moscow, one of my friends said something interesting regarding alcohol consumption. He said, "You know for sure that you have become an alcoholic the day you are drinking by yourself." His clever insight underscored the root problem of alcohol abuse: it is primarily a social disease of loneliness. That is why the only effective methods of treating alcohol addiction are based on community support groups.

Community groups curb the addictiveness of games, because they give room for meaningful and rewarding human interactions. They connect people around a common interest. One of the best ways to protect yourself from virtual dangers is to play with a group of people that you know in the physical world. The benefits of gaming will increase, and the potential negative effects of gaming will decrease. Part of the reason why this works so well is the scheduling difficulty of getting a group of busy people together for leisure.

Find a game buddy who is a mature independent adult. It is difficult to synchronize schedules of two or more people to play obsessively. If you have a friend or a group of friends to play regularly with, you may find yourself managing your time much better. Wisely chosen community group can also shield you from pornographic and violent or otherwise-questionable content. Some temptations are much easier to resist in the proximity of other people. If you play the same games together, other players in your group will know what you have done and how many times. We do not want to leave an impression of being a maniac or a pervert with our close friends so our awareness of morality heightens when friends are nearby. For some individuals, spending all their game time with a community group may be mandatory for those reasons.

Encourage your children to play with their siblings and friends rather than by themselves. An easy way to do this is to give them a major bonus to their virtual time allowance, if they play with a community rather than in isolation. This will solve several problems at once. Those gaming sessions will be easier to supervise. Your children will have opportunities to build friendships and learn how to share. If it is a large group of friends and they take turns playing, they will remember that they are hungry and thirsty during the breaks and take better care of their physical needs. Having adventures together creates a strong bond and gives children common experiences with their friends.

Maintain One-World Priority

Regardless of how much time we might choose to devote to virtual worlds, every person must embrace this basic rule: one-world priority. It is the core commitment to value everything in the physical world above anything that may exist or occur in a virtual world. Things that happen in a virtual world must never be allowed to influence our schedules or cause us to postpone or neglect anything that happens in the physical world.

This rudimentary principle is usually the first one to be violated. Virtual worlds can alter sleeping schedules, cause us to miss deadlines for school or work, divide our attention, scatter our concentration, and even cause us to forget to eat. One-world priority does not come naturally to us, because by default we tend to value personal entertainment above all else even at our own peril. Selfishness and carelessness are natural; selflessness and responsibility have to be taught and maintained.

As we discussed in the section on discipline, stay away from games that do not have a pause button. The majority of multiplayer games do not have a pause button, because other players are involved in the game at the same time. But there are often mechanics in place that can work like a pause button. For example, some games have safety zones, where you can leave your character temporarily while you stepped away from the computer. Other games might consist of rounds that are several minutes long, allowing you to go on break in-between rounds or sit one out.

Commit yourself to leaving the virtual world every time something comes up in the physical world. It is not a bad idea to tape this slogan to your monitor: "Only one world actually exists." Games you should definitely avoid are the ones that require your full undivided attention for an extended period of time or force you to organize your schedule around events that happen in the virtual world. Those kinds of virtual worlds violate the priority of the physical world, because they begin to dictate your physical activity based on your virtual activity. Some of the Massive Multiplayer Online games have the worst track record in this regard, because they frequently involve thousands of players in scheduled activities.

One-world priority can be difficult to observe in competitive settings. Do not try to be competitive in virtual worlds unless you are actually very gifted and trying to win a real competition with a monetary prize. There is always an eight-year-old South Korean kid out there that that will beat you embarrassingly in the game, post your humiliation on Facebook, and tag you in the post. It is not worth your time to work hard to be the best in an online game or the first on the scoreboard. Focus your effort to areas in your life in which you are gifted. You are not gifted at computer games, and the ones who are gifted have to practice for at least forty hours a week to maintain competitive edge.

Losing in a computer game does not make you a loser in life, as long as you are winning prizes that actually matter – honoring God, providing for your family, and having good friends. Only play a game if the game itself is fun for you. Do not play it if it becomes a way of attaining fun, especially if the achievement you are chasing is a moving target set relative to the performance of other players. Remember that only one world actually exists.

Set a Dare Limit

Set a personal "dare limit" for virtual worlds and stick with it. Brainstorm a list of things that you would be willing to try for the sake of experiencing something new. Start by making a list of things that you would dare to try in the physical world. Almost every person has a definite dare limit, especially if they are responsible for the well-being of others. You may be willing to try sky diving, but few people would realistically be willing to test a new flight device, that had never been used before, by jumping off a cliff with it. Many people would be willing to try new exotic foods, but few people would inject themselves with a completely unknown substance. Some may dare to travel to an uninhabitable island, but few would venture into a war zone out of curiosity. Everybody has a limit of what they would dare to do, if they had an opportunity.

When you make this list, it is alright to be slightly ridiculous. Think about every aspect of your life, and what would you be willing to gamble in search of excitement. This exercise is fun to do with your entire family. You may even add things that are impossible to this list. Group up the list items to make the list shorter. What is the most ridiculous thing you would eat, if you could eat anything? What wouldn't you eat? What would be the most ridiculous thing that you would do to your appearance? What wouldn't you do? What places would you visit? What places would you not visit?

The answers will vary wildly from person to person, but they will help create a moral grid for exploring virtual worlds. If you wouldn't be willing to try something in the physical world, it is best not to try it in the virtual world. Otherwise, your conscience may be violated bringing feelings of guilt and shame. A human feeling of guilt is like pain, because it informs us of danger. Suppressing guilt numbs the conscience and limits opportunities for personal growth. If you are feeling guilt, you should stop the game.

Compiling a dare list helps you define a line proactively that you personally should not cross in your exploration of the virtual worlds. Devote more attention to brainstorming scenarios involving criminal or immoral activity. You may watch a movie involving a criminal activity, but taking part in one as an accomplice or even an instigator in a virtual world takes a moral dilemma to a whole new level. Would you smuggle drugs and sell them to minors? Would you torture a person if they had information you really wanted? Would you attack a person in their sleep? If you have doubts or moral reservations about anything, scratch it off the dare list. It is easy to conjure excuses to satisfy curiosity in pursuit of thrills, but doing so will numb and erode your conscience over time.

Use this dare limit to shop for games. If you have on your list "I would not dare to shoot a stranger in the face," it is best for you not to buy games in which you are expected to shoot complete strangers in the face. Doing this exercise with your community group or family will lead to many good discussions, and making one big list together will keep you away from the idiosyncrasies that blind you. You might be surprised how many things that you would dare to try others might find completely repulsive. Invite a war veteran to your home to share his combat memories with your family. Even if you continue to play shooting games after this visit, I guarantee you that your attitude toward those games will change profoundly.

CHAPTER 5

VIRTUAL WORLDS IN FAMILY CONTEXT

"All happy families resemble one another;
every unhappy family is unhappy in its own way." – Leo Tolstoy

Computer games compound typical family tensions by creating new battle fronts, but they can also help bring families together and even assist parents in child rearing process. Virtual worlds can serve as training grounds and playing grounds for the whole family, if every member makes an effort to exercise intentional care. The subject of parenting and computer games deserves its own book. Thankfully, Scott Steinberg already wrote an excellent one titled "The Modern Parent's Guide to Kids and Video Games" (www.videogamesandkids.com). If you are specifically concerned with the subject of parenting, you should get his book. There is really no point for me to try to duplicate Steinberg's effort on gaming and parenting, since you can download an electronic version of his superb book for free from the book's website, so I will simply provide some additional insight and highlight a few recommendations that you might not be able to find elsewhere.

Gaming is often a battlefield of contention between children and parents. Children always think that parents are too restrictive and unwilling to understand their unquenchable need for virtual world participation. Parents always think that they are constantly pressed to compromise boundaries that they set no matter how generous and open and understanding they may try to be towards their children. Get ready to have to battle against one certainty: persistent and defiant disobedience. In the past, parents have often forbid their children to play computer games altogether in order to avoid having to deal with this problem. Prohibition of electronic entertainment is still a viable option for young kids living in your home in isolation from other kids. If they ever get out of the house on their own or have a cell phone or their own computer, forbidding them to play is not a sustainable parenting strategy.

This problem grows double if you are parenting boys. Games are primarily marketed to them. Furthermore, modern system of education, leftover from the industrial age of mass secular indoctrination, is prone to frustrate and bore boys. There is nothing more unnatural and deflating than putting a young male behind a desk, forcing him to sit in a row with others and listening quietly to one person speak. You might have more luck putting a dog cone collar on a tiger! For boys, virtual worlds can quickly become a preferred alternative to the drudgery of everyday schooling. They are so much more existing and filled with risk and adventure. Below are some suggestions that will make a difference in your family.

The exact amount of time that children should be allowed to play can be difficult to determine. The American Academy of Pediatrics recommends about one hour of gaming in virtual worlds per day. This recommendation is a good place to start, but children are quite different in personality and inclinations. Some mature fast and some take a while. Some exhibit violence and hostility, and others can be passive and personable. Generally, it is a good idea to reward self-regulation with freedom. If your child is making more mature choices and manages his or her time wisely, it will benefit them to have an ability to manage more of their time in a limited way on their own. To test their ability to exercise self-control, allow them one night of free time during the work week, which they may choose to spend on their hobbies. If homework and chores continue to get done without direct parental oversight, the child is showing signs of maturity. Being honest and taking responsibility is also a great sign of maturity. Celebrate with your kids and reward them, when they step up to adult expectations.

Parents naturally do this all the time. If a child makes good grades, you let them hang out with friends a little bit longer. If they get a summer job, you let them get a cellphone or start teaching them how to drive. Follow a similar pattern with electronic entertainment, especially if you see them begin to discipline themselves. If they quit playing games on their own to finish homework, even though they could continue to play by household rules, it is a good sign that your child is maturing.

They will disappoint you frequently, and those times should not be viewed as instances of parental failure. Rather, you should think of those frequent occasions as opportunities to instruct and to nurture. Be stern and gentle. Explain main reasons for changes when you adjust rules or apply discipline through punishment and restriction. Discipline can be especially difficult to instill among siblings. It is hard to stay fair with reward and punishment, because each child requires personalized discipline due to having unique personality refracted by gender, age, and birth order. Fairness is impossible to attain, but reaching for some degree of justice is both a worthy and a realistic goal. Teaching the difference between the two at a young age will prepare them for adulthood.

If your children are asking for permission to spend more time in virtual worlds, it may be unwise to give them more time indiscriminately. They may have a particular game in mind already, which they really want to play. Increased attachment to one virtual world could be an early sign of a danger. Instead of increasing their total screen time, a better solution is to give them extra time to spend on more than one game or more time on certain kinds of games. For example, you may allow additional time devoted to games that are educational with low degree of violence. This will help your child understand your concerns and your desire to protect them. Try this approach first and monitor the results before giving greater freedom. This way you will also teach them the principle of selectivity.

Learn How to Play

If you do not play computer games, find some games that you might like and learn how to play them. Yes, I am talking to you! You can show another person that you care about them by maintaining continuous presence in their life. In the past, keeping proximity was required for safety and prosperity. Parents passed their businesses down to their children, and the well-being of families was tied to proper management of generational inheritance. Industrial age made this mandatory closeness optional. The benefit of this freedom is the opportunity to develop deep and meaningful relationships unhindered by economic coercion. The challenge of this freedom is in the increasing amount of effort required to maintain close relationships. You really have to go out of your way to break from the routine and to spend time with your family.

Virtual worlds can be seen as another obstacle in the way of building relationships, but they can also encourage healthy interactions and bring families closer together. Children naturally play. They seldom need encouragement in that area. Parents are highly suspicious of video games, because they do not see the point of allowing kids near them. Perhaps previous chapters have helped alleviate some of those fears. There is also a higher and more important reason for playing than just spending time together. Computer games can help parents become incarnate in the world of their children.

Incarnational presence is a powerful expression of love. Parents practice it with their children without realizing it by assuming pretend roles for their amusement. Children assume pretend roles in almost all their games, but they especially enjoy it when their parents participate. It is hard to explain why. It is even more curious that when children invite parents to play with them, they usually offer them a particular kind of role that they thought of in advance. "Daddy, you will be the policeman!" Or, "I will be a doctor and you will be my patient." If you play your part, the children will be greatly amused. Then, another important thing happens. A few minutes into the game, they are looking for guidance from you! They really do not know how the game is supposed to go. They were making it up as they go, and now it is your turn to continue. Even in a made up world, they are looking at you as a leader and a guide.

You know where I am going with this. Learn how to play video games – enter their world. It does not really matter if you are good. Keeping an intentional incarnational presence in their lives makes all the difference in the long run. In this process, your personality and ethics are communicated through the game by your example. You will teach children how to play correctly by showing them how to do it. Children will learn how to play by watching you play, and through this they are learning how to live. Having adventures together builds fond memories. Games can be difficult to learn, but some are good for all ages and easy to learn. If you have never played anything, try Minecraft (www.minecraft.net). Watch a few videos online of other people playing it if you get stuck.

There is another supremely important reason to learn how

to play. If you play the games your children play, you will be able screen those games for morally questionable content for them. You do not have to do this with every game they play, but certain ones may require a thorough screening. One of my friends read the entire "Harry Potter" series of novels for kids, because he was concerned about the presence of witchcraft and magic in those popular novels and how it may affect his children. He decided to allow his daughter to read them, but he told his son to wait for two years. His children respected this decision much, because the father invested considerable effort and care to screen the books for them. Sometimes being a responsible parent calls for walking up a nature trail first to check it for snakes.

Watch Reviews

Virtual worlds are steadily becoming the primary form of art. They will continue to dominate the entertainment market, and they are already penetrating the mainstream pop culture. Remaining ignorant about games will eventually put you out of touch with your own culture. Fortunately, keeping yourself up to date is easier than it has ever been even if you are strapped for time.

Games and movies both have trailers. For movies, trailers are the most potent form of advertisement. Few people read a movie review before they go watch a movie, although they might check a movie critic score. Trailers can be misleading, especially when it comes to comedies. How often have you gone to see a comedy just to realize that all the really funny parts were already in the trailer? Unlike movies, computer games are rarely advertised by means of trailers, because this form of advertisement is not nearly as effective for games. A trailer does not communicate what the virtual world "feels like." It does not capture the depth and variety of choices that players have to make.

The two most effective forms of advertisement for games are demo-versions and reviews. A demo is a greatly reduced version of the virtual world downloadable for free. Presumably, if players download the demo and like playing it for thirty minutes, they will want to buy the full version of the game. Demos can be helpful and fun, but they usually require a few hours to explore. Reviews, on the other hand, are usually short articles or video clips commenting on the content and quality of the game. They take only five minutes and they can tell you most of what you need to know. Reviews by commercial and independent press literally make and break games in terms of their success, because international gaming community is so closely knit and organized.

Therefore, the quality and fidelity of game reviews is fairly consistent between different press organizations, although some of them hesitate to slam weak games that are backed by major companies. I recommend watching video reviews, because they are short and to the point. They also show footage of the gameplay. Finding a video review on the Internet is easy by typing the name of the game followed by the words "video review" into a search engine. When you no longer know what your children or friends are talking about, look for a video review. It will give you enough information to empower you to listen with comprehension and to share your thoughts intelligently.

If you do not remember anything else from this book, remember this piece of smart consumer advice: never buy a video game without, at the very least, watching a video review. By spending five minutes, you will have an idea if it contains major questionable content and if it has a good overarching message. A lot of games have glitches and unforgivable flaws that will be criticized in the video review. If you plan to play the game yourself, watching the video review will not spoil it for you. A typical game is designed for 15-25 hours of gameplay, and a clip of five minutes will rarely contain anything but the introduction to the story. If you are planning to buy the game, invite your family to watch one of the reviews with you. Family discussion that follows will help you spend your money wisely and will teach young members of the household how to make this kind of a decision.

Lead Social Interactions

Virtual worlds are simultaneously the most entertaining and the most dangerous when it comes to social interactions between players. The best way to protect your family from dangerous social interactions is to become a social leader in virtual worlds. Taking charge does not require overbearing commitment or time investment. Leadership is providing initiative and maintaining communication. You may never be good at playing games or even find them interesting, but you can still provide social leadership.

Knowing too little about virtual worlds should not deter you from a leadership role. A good leader is never the most intelligent, gifted, or even charismatic person. Rather, a good leader finds ways to empower others and help them work together. The less you know about games, the more you will have to rely on your friends and children. Let them educate you on the basics and provide initiative in harmony with their input. There are many practical ways of doing this.

Host a gaming party for your friends and their kids. Provide food and drink. Enlist others to help you pick games. You can start small with events just for children, because they are easy to please. You will earn much respect in their eyes for hosting a game night, even if you personally do not participate. Connect with other parents and create a mailing list to share articles and ideas on this subject. Form a group on Facebook. Gaming parties do not have to be frequent or even regular to make a difference. They will provide entertainment and serve as a model for proper socializing. Warm environment gives children an ability to establish a sense of comfort and safety by which they can weigh future virtual interactions.

Sponsor a clan or a competition league. Players bond and form groups naturally called clans or guilds. You can validate those groups by investing into them. If there is a group of children that play together regularly, offer to help them set up and pay the fees for a clan website. Offer to pay for their bus tickets for local league competitions and go with them. Your credibility will go through the roof, because most of the other groups of kids will not have an "official sponsor." And as a sponsor, you will have some say in where they go and what they do and how often they practice.

Endure Disobedience

You will often be tempted to give in or give up to the schemes of tiny expert manipulators. Do not yield to disobedience! It is your responsibility before God and your duty before mankind to raise your children as responsible and socially adept citizens. Sagging of parental discipline is a form of neglect and un-love. Discipline without love or wisdom can also easily go wrong and produce an effect opposite of the intended. Be loving and patient in all your communication with a disobedient child. Ask more questions than you make statements, and let them know that you are talking to them in order to allow them to participate in their own discipline process. Teach them how to apologize and repent in order to partially mitigate their punishment, and give them clear opportunity to do so. Instruct them that every choice has consequences, but that decisions made in judgment can also be reviewed and softened if there is willingness to change over time.

Never make disciplinary threats. Children will eventually start making their own threats, and they will constantly challenge your words as a way of asserting independence. By "disciplinary threat" I mean situations when you are trying to get them to change their behavior by promising them punishment if they do not. Lay down household rules ahead of time with the kinds of disciplinary punishments children should expect, and when they are violating them be ready to immediately apply the rules. In other words, delayed discipline and rules made up in the moment have limited effectiveness. If you are unable to punish them immediately, let them know that they have broken an established rule and they will answer for it at the first convenient moment.

Pick your battles to conserve your willpower and emotional strength. Parenting is not easy, and it will wear on you. Specific household rules, written out ahead of time, will help you conserve energy. Invest time into creating, reviewing, and teaching them to your children. Give them opportunities to contribute to the discussions of household rules. Even if you weigh their input only at 1%, your act of listening will communicate concern and love to them. Keep household rules easy to understand and to follow, emphasizing that lying and disrespecting parents are the worst offenses. Most importantly, restrict your own entertainment in some meaningful way to give an example of self-discipline and sacrifice for greater good. Household entertainment rules should not be just for children (see Appendix for an example).

Pursue full mutual agreement with your spouse on the questions of discipline. There is nothing more damaging to household discipline than open disagreement between spouses regarding it. Children get sneaky and try to find the more favorably disposed or lenient parent. Your ability to synchronize with your spouse will test the depth of your relationship constantly. It is an impossible feat to reach 100% agreement, but you can give a strong impression of agreement by keeping disagreement private between just you and your spouse.

CHAPTER 6

CONCLUSION

"Baseball, it is said, is only a game. True. And the Grand Canyon is only a hole in Arizona. Not all holes, or games, are created equal." – George Will

We should expect a greater variety of virtual words in the near future. Possibilities are limited only by human imagination. Gaming innovators have been experimenting restlessly with virtual worlds and they are achieving great rates of success. Game genres are combined in unforeseen ways to create interesting and unusual worlds. Augmented reality games, which project virtual world on the physical, is a rather curious development. They give new purpose and meaning to human interactions to facilitate physical adventures with the help of the virtual. For instance, the computer game "Ingress" uses cellphone GPS technology to encourage group sight-seeing of physical landmarks through mock scavenger hunts involving thousands of people. In essence, this game is "Capture the Flag" wrapped in a clever science fiction story that encourages exploration and adventure of your city by creating a bridge into the virtual world.

Another developing trend is the gradual merging of virtual

and physical economies. Virtual items and currency have been traded on the Internet for many years. The volume of those transactions is growing astronomically. There are cases when the value of the virtual items surpasses the value of their physical equivalents. Virtual scams and thefts are already common. Some virtual economies are so massive and so developed that they attract professional and academic experts, and even thieves, for purposes of market research and even generating profit through trade and other means. A notorious example is the theft of over $30,000 USD of virtual currency by means of a Ponzi scheme from other players in game Eve Online. This case is far from being an isolated instance.

Rapid innovation and the inevitable collision between virtual and physical world economies ensure that virtual worlds will become more beneficial and at the same time more dangerous. Increased complexity and raised stakes of the decisions you have to make will not diminish one bit. I hope this book has given you a grid which will help you recognize and face your challenges and make your own good decisions. I also hope that some of the given suggestions will serve as decent examples by which you will be able to construct your own ways of protecting yourself and your family. Be vigilant, and be mindful of others. Things that may seem completely harmless for you may be devastating to the less experienced or more impressionable members of your household.

I would like to end the book with a few final recommendations specifically for readers that have almost never played computer games. There will always be a segment of society like that. Some are from very poor families in which even children had to go to work every day, some are from broken families in which staying at home was hazardous, and others are from radical religious families in which entertainment and technology were considered Satan's ruse to subvert God's plan. If you picked up this book, you have probably realized that maintaining seclusion is becoming unfeasible. Even if you stayed away from technology, it did not stay away from you. It found its way into your pocket. And now that it made a little nest there, you realized that it came loaded to the brim with games, and now your kids got their hands on it.

If you are new to virtual worlds, take it slow and do not rush to try everything and learn everything at once. Talk to people who already play first before spending money. Never buy new video games when they are released. They are not worth the typical price tag of $60. Most games are full of glitches when they first come out, and if you just wait for one year you will get the exact same game of better quality for at least half the cost. Rent and borrow games when you can, and stick to older games. For most new games there is a better old game of the same kind available for much lower price, if you ask around. Stay away from Xbox and Playstation (and Mac) – you will lose money on those systems because their markets are rigged for inflating prices in unethical ways.

The best places to buy games are Good Old Games store (www.gog.com) and Steam store (www.steampowered.com) during holiday and summer sales, and I would not pay more than $10 per game. If the game costs more than $10, just wait for it to go on sale. Most of them will drop to that price within about eight months. You do not have to own a powerful computer to play most games. It is better to buy one family computer in $400-600 range, built with AMD APU technology, if you have children (see Appendix). Slower computer will naturally restrict your family to older and cleaner games, which will ease your task as a parent initially. It is not a good idea to let children have their own computer before they start writing their own papers on adult subjects.

Gaming apocalypse does not have to be the end of the world for you or your family. Virtual reality is transforming our lives at least as much as the printing press transformed medieval Europe 500 years ago. And while the Pope at the time thought that putting the Bible into every person's hand would bring about the "book apocalypse," it did not turn out as bad as he thought. We printed evil books and we printed good books. The evil books are wasting away together with the people enslaved by them. And the good books remain, which we now call classical literature. Become a part of building a legacy for future generations in this new realm, and I hope that this book helps you stay on the right path.

APPENDIX A

SAMPLE HOUSEHOLD RULES

1. Children can suggest games, but they can only play games approved by parents.

2. Games can only be played after work is done, or certain games can be played in 20 minute breaks between work.

3. Each playing session must not be longer than 1-2 hours.

4. Gaming and internet are allowed only between 2pm and 7pm.

5. Gaming and internet are not allowed when you are alone or with a closed door.

6. Each day, only 2-3 hours can be spent on electronic entertainment total, which includes television. If friends come over to play, game time can be increased by permission.

7. Permission for more game time can be obtained on some days if both parents agree.

8. Parents will take the game away, if questionable content is discovered in it.

9. Breaking the household rules will result in discipline which will include one or more of the following temporary measures: reduction of game time, confiscation of electronic equipment, suspension of internet access, ban on certain games, blocking of all numbers except family on cellphone.

10. Lying, subverting restrictions or malicious tempering of equipment results in double penalty.

APPENDIX B

HEALTH TIPS FOR GAMERS

1. Always have a water bottle next to you. Contigo Autoseal (www.gocontigo.com) is one of the best, because it prevents spills. If your urine is not clear like tap water, you are not drinking enough.

2. Make sure that your chair is comfortable and that you are always sitting straight.

3. Take regular breaks which involve activities that force you to focus your eyes further away than your screen.

4. Walking is almost as beneficial as running to your health and requires a lot less effort. Walking for 30 minutes each day mitigates the majority of risks associated with sedentary life style.

5. Generally speaking, any food that comes in a box, package, can, plastic bottle, or a wrapper is not good for you. Flee it like the plague!

6. If you tend to play more than one hour per day, play different games and different kinds of games on purpose to reduce the risk of compulsive addiction.

7. Consistent and regular sleep is sacred. If you tend to stay up, do so consistently in the same hours.

APPENDIX C

FAMILY COMPUTER

For most situations family computer will cost around $400-600. The following setup will play 90% of the games decently and double as an office machine working smoother than most laptops. Building a computer yourself will save you some money, and putting parts together is easy once you watch a few videos of another person doing it on Youtube. If you have never built a computer before, it is best to spend some time with Tek Syndycate (www.teksyndicate.com) or enlist help from a person who has. You can also buy a used one, but only do so if you personally know the person selling it to you. Dell and other major retailers will have good selections, but they will try to sell you more power than you really need.

Minimum Hardware

- Motherboard: Socket FM2 with on-board audio.
- Processor: APU AMD A6-6400K Richland 3.9GHz or better.
- Video Card: Not needed, because the AMD APU technology includes it.
- Memory: 8 GB (2x4GB Modules) 1600MHz
- Hard-disk: Western Digital Caviar Blue 500 GB 7200 RPM

Minimum Software

For an operating system, Windows 7 or 8 will still give you the greatest flexibility in what your computer can do for the best price. LibreOffice (www.libreoffice.org) is the best office suite by far and it is completely free. Backup Maker Free Edition (www.ascomp.de) and Dropbox (www.dropbox.com) together will keep your files safe. RescueTime (www.rescuetime.com) sends you weekly reports by electronic mail on how the time on your computer was spent and which applications were used the most.

Software for Kids

KeePass (www.keepass.info) will keep all your passwords organized and safe from children and hackers, and it works marvelously together with Dropbox to synchronize all your passwords between all your devices. Qustudio (www.qustodio.com) is one of the best parental control systems that will let you set strict boundaries on computer use and enforce them.

Use Internet search engine to find out what other parents are doing with children your age. There are thousands of great suggestions on forums. Some parents use a ticketing system by giving out play time cards regularly and as rewards. This can work well with older children, allowing them to save up game time and learn how to manage it on their own.

ABOUT THE AUTHOR

Dima Kotik is a historian on a quest to inspire others to reinvest their lives into efforts that last. He challenges his readers to find meaning and identity in Christ by reflecting on the past, and to discover a new sense of purpose and significance in continuing Christ's legacy. Dima challenges conventional practices and thought patterns with fresh and daring insights honed in thoughtful exploration of history.

Dima studied Church history and theology at Moody Bible Institute in Chicago and Dallas Theological Seminary. He is especially interested in history of missiology, mysticism, and military technology. In his spare time, he enjoys writing software and practicing martial arts, and, like all Russians, sometimes he dances sitting down.

www.ingramcontent.com/pod-product-compliance
Lightning Source LLC
Chambersburg PA
CBHW061020050326
40689CB00012B/2698